John Pisano's
JAZZ**GUITAR**COMPING
MASTERCLASS

Go Beyond Rhythm Guitar & Discover the Chord Comping Lines of a True Jazz Virtuoso

JOHN**PISANO**

With Tim Pettingale

FUNDAMENTAL**CHANGES**

John Pisano's Jazz Guitar Comping Masterclass

Go Beyond Rhythm Guitar & Discover the Chord Comping Lines of a True Jazz Virtuoso

ISBN: 978-1-78933-214-8

Published by **www.fundamental-changes.com**

www.fundamental-changes.com

Cover Image Copyright: Author photo by Bob Barry, **www.jazzography.com**, used by permission.

Special thanks from John Pisano and Fundamental Changes to Rogerio Peixoto, for your invaluable help in bringing this project together.

Transcription by Daryl Kellie

Contents

Introduction

My background

My first recollection of being attracted to the sound of the guitar was hearing the theme tune to a 1939 radio show called *Blondie*. The theme was played by a string quartet, but it had a solo guitar break. I sat on the floor with my ear to the radio every week and waited to hear that guitar solo. I later found out that George Van Eps had written it.

The first time I recall being struck by a sense of *rhythm* was a couple of years later when I heard Carmen Miranda and José Carioca and his "Bando Carioca". He played the cavaquinho (a Portuguese stringed instrument resembling a small classical guitar). My Dad also played guitar, and his brother played banjo, and they would play all the standard tunes of the day, so I grew up with the sound of the guitar in my ears. It intrigued me long before I thought about playing the instrument.

My first teacher was Mrs. Cora Fellows, who was a teacher of "fretted instruments", in 1944. Of all the things she taught me, the piece of advice that I remember to this day is, "Let the pick do the work!" She wanted me to learn to relax and not squeeze the pick, which creates tension. She was a wonderful teacher.

While studying with Mrs. Fellows, I discovered Django Reinhardt. I spent many hours listening to his music, working things out by ear, analyzing what he was doing and memorizing some of his solos. Soon my friends had nicknamed me "Django"! What I got from him was an understanding of rhythm, energy, phrasing and melodic content. He was a great composer as well as a genius on the guitar.

My next important teacher was Chuck Wayne. It was around the time when Charlie Parker and bebop came into the jazz world and Chuck was playing with Charlie, George Shearing and many others on the scene. Influenced by Charlie, Chuck is credited as the first player to translate bebop onto the guitar. Chuck had a four-note system for chord voicings that became valuable to me, but he also introduced me to the technique he called "back picking", meaning to sweep across the strings in both directions. Chuck was an outstanding influence on me, and people often told me that I sounded like him.

In 1951 I joined the US Air Force and played in the Air Force Band in Washington, D.C. for four years. At that time, the guitarist Charlie Byrd was living in D.C. He was a student of Andrés Segovia and I thought this was a good opportunity for me to study classical guitar, so I took lessons with Charlie for a while. He helped me to improve my picking hand fingerstyle technique.

In 1953 I remember purchasing an album featuring Bud Shank and Laurindo Almeida. This introduced me to the music of Brazil and its rhythms, and I became proficient at playing this music. This paid off well, as I ended up working and recording with Sergio Mendes and other Brazilian artists like Dori Caymmi, Toninho Horta and Ivan Lins.

In 1954, while still in the Air Force, I got the chance to meet the guitarist Johnny Smith who was appearing in town. We met on several more occasions and became friends, and Johnny really liked my original compositions. Johnny taught me to always practice things slowly, with a clean, even tone. He insisted I should never practice anything fast – even though he was known for his amazing facility on guitar. It's worth holding onto this bit of wisdom. If you don't learn to play something cleanly at a slow speed, you'll just end up playing it faster badly.

By 1956 I was out of the service and had moved back to New York. I enrolled in the Manhattan School of Music, but before I started the course, I flew out to Los Angeles to join the Chico Hamilton Quintet, replacing Jim Hall. I stayed with Chico until 1958. That year, the guitarist Billy Bean came to Los Angeles and we ended up making two guitar duet albums for Decca: *Take Your Pick* and *Makin' It*. Years later these recordings were revived and released on the String Jazz album based in the UK. Billy was a major influence on me.

I met Lenny Breau in 1960 and we played together often and exchanged many ideas. Lenny was a guitar genius. Still wanting to learn more, in 1962 I enrolled in Los Angeles City College to study harmony and composition with Leonard Stein and during this time I also studied classical guitar with Celendonio Romero. I also met up with George Van Eps, taking private lessons with him, and we developed a great friendship. I received a lot of help from George, as well as guitar greats like Bob Bain and Al Viola. Two other major influences on me around this time were Peggy Lee and Herb Alpert.

A year later, in 1963, I met Joe Pass. At the time he was in recovery at Synanon in Santa Monica, California. I visited him there on several occasions and later played on his *For Django* album. We became close friends and went on to do many recordings and concert tours together.

One more name must be mentioned… I first met Ted Greene (author of the famous book *Chord Chemistry*) in 1986, and he became a dear friend. I studied with Ted until around 2005 because his knowledge of the guitar was so vast, and I felt privileged to be able to receive some of that knowledge and insight.

All of these people greatly added to my musical life and I will always be deeply grateful to them.

How to use this book

Just as jazz guitar soloists will "hear" different melodic lines over a set of changes then play them, I hear different *harmonic movements* in the chord progression. My aim is always to provide a solid foundation for the soloist, but also to add interest, light and shade; to keep the rhythm flowing and keep the audience engaged. Music is a fluid thing and much of the excitement of jazz comes from the spontaneous interaction of the musicians. Jazz isn't a speech – it's a musical conversation.

In order to communicate what we want to say on guitar, however, we need to have a good grasp of the language. When we learn a new language, we usually begin with some useful phrases that will help us navigate certain situations. What I've set out to give you in this book are a collection of "chord phrases" that work really well in a variety of situations. You can learn them as phrases in their own right, but they should also be a springboard for your own exploration and creativity.

Jazz improvisation is an "in the moment" thing, and theory is the last thing we're thinking about on the bandstand. We often play things just because we happen upon a sound we like, then worry about the theory later. This is fine! To that end, I've kept the theory to a minimum – this is more about learning the language of jazz guitar comping – but I will show you how you can develop these ideas for yourself along the way.

Guitar players often get stuck in a rut, so I hope you'll find some ideas here that you may not have thought of. They are tried and tested melodic movements that *just work*.

As well as a collection of useful shorter lines over common chord progressions, there are several longer etudes here, where I play several choruses of well-known jazz standards. Whenever you discover a new idea, it's important to apply it straight away to tunes you know. This way, you'll absorb it into your playing much more quickly and it will become a part of your chord vocabulary.

I trust that you enjoy this book and I hope it enriches your playing.

Have fun!

John Pisano
August 2021

Get the Audio

The audio files for this book are available to download for free from **www.fundamental-changes.com.** The link is in the top right-hand corner. Simply select this book title from the drop-down menu and follow the instructions to get the audio.

We recommend that you download the files directly to your computer, not to your tablet, and extract them there before adding them to your media library. You can then put them on your tablet, iPod or burn them to CD. On the download page there is a help PDF and we also provide technical support via the contact form.

For over 350 free guitar lessons with videos check out:

www.fundamental-changes.com

Join our free Facebook Community of Cool Musicians

www.facebook.com/groups/fundamentalguitar

Tag us for a share on Instagram: **FundamentalChanges**

Chapter One: Strategies for Creating Comping Movements

By Tim Pettingale

John Pisano's journey into learning chord moves began with his guitar teacher, Chuck Wayne. Chuck had devised his own unique system of playing that did away with the "cowboy" chords most of us learnt when we first picked up the guitar in favor of a more pianistic approach. One of the great benefits of his system was that it mapped out chord voicings across the neck, giving many options for creating comping movements.

After studying with Chuck, and referring to books like George Van Eps' *Harmonic Mechanisms*, John developed his style by soaking up as much music as he could, absorbing and applying the things he liked. Inspiration came from copying the harmonic moves of other guitar players and pianists, but also of orchestral arrangers like the master, Gil Evans.

Over the years, John has played with many of the jazz guitar greats and was influenced by players like Johnny Smith, Joe Pass, Jim Hall, Tal Farlow and later, Lenny Breau and Ed Bickert – all of whom had their own strategies for playing chordal passages. John picked up different ideas from each of them and these influences combined to develop his own unique voice on the instrument.

In this book, John passes on some of his favorite moves and ways of navigating chord changes that break away from the routine choices. Before we get to those, however, we need to lay a foundation from which you can build *your own* comping chops. In this chapter, we're going to break down some of the ideas John uses, so you can see how to apply these ideas yourself. Treat this section as a primer to help you understand and explore some of the conceptual ideas that John uses before we learn his actual chordal approaches from Chapter Two onwards.

What is comping?

Many guitarists consider rhythm playing and comping to be one and the same thing, but actually they're different. Rhythm is playing a repeating pattern with different accents. Comping is the art of combining harmonic and rhythmic phrases in such a way that it complements and inspires a soloist.

In comping, the guitarist will play what can be called "chord phrases", which have more in common with the kind of arrangements a big band plays, distilled down onto guitar. Like the sound of a big band, guitar comping can include walking basslines, countermelodies, partial chords and single-line passages where appropriate.

To develop your comping technique, there are two essential skills you need to work on, which will help you to master the fretboard and grow your comping vocabulary.

1. The ability to embellish chords.

2. The ability to play chord voicings across the neck.

In the coming pages we'll explore some different ways of embellishing chords and giving them movement and direction.

Embellishing chords

To embellish a chord simply means to enhance it by adding *movement*. This movement can be created by...

- Moving one or more of the chord's tones up or down

- Combining it with other chord shapes from the same parent scale

- A combination of the two

Let's see how this concept works using just one chord.

Imagine you have four bars of G Major to play over and you want to come up with something interesting. Listen to John comping and you'll often hear him play through many chord shapes, even though there is only *one chord* written on the lead sheet. Here is a method to generate those different shapes.

First, take a look at this common Gmaj7 chord shape in third position.

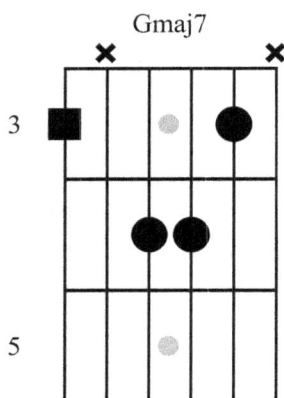

It's what you might typically play if you saw Gmaj7 on a chord chart. In order to open up possibilities for creating "chord phrases", we can use this chord's parent scale, G Major, as our source.

John actually tends to think more in terms of *scales* than *chords* and a lot of his comping magic comes from knowing the intervals of a scale on different strings and being able to build chord voicings on each note.

The G Major scale contains the notes G, A, B, C, D, E, F#.

We can build simple chord structures on each of these notes to *harmonize* the scale. This means to stack intervals of a 3rd (every other note) on top of a root note.

So, the Gmaj7 chord above is constructed G (root), B (3rd), D (5th) and F# (7th).

To free up a finger that can add embellishment notes, we can omit the 5th and play a three-note voicing that contains just the root (G), 3rd (B) and 7th (F#).

If we build similar root, 3rd and 7th voicings on *every* note of the G Major scale, it generates the following set of shapes. Play them in sequence and you'll hear the G Major scale in chord form.

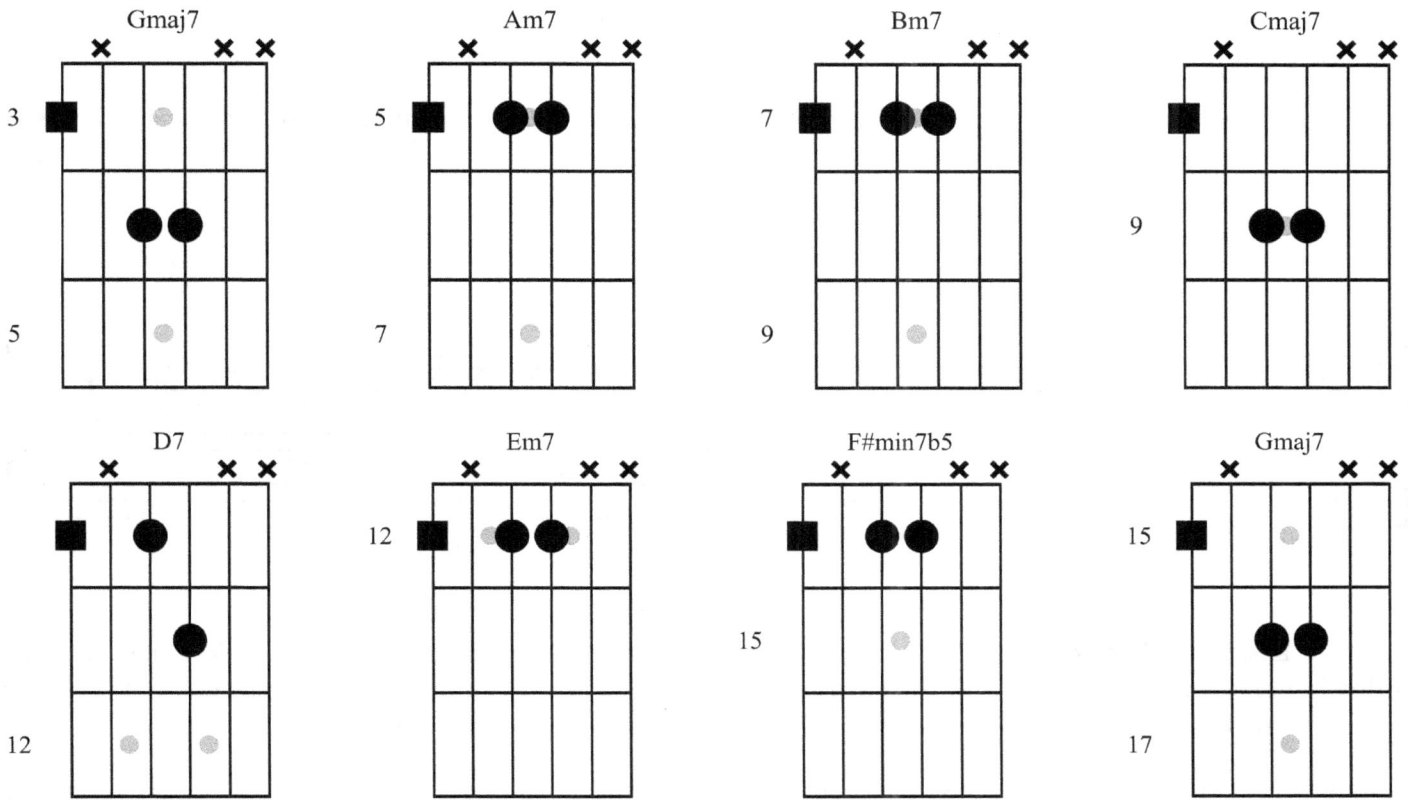

These shapes are our starting point for creating some comping vocabulary.

How we finger the shapes is important when it comes to embellishing them. Instinctively, you may want to play them using fingers 1, 2 and 3 with the first finger fretting the root note.

Instead, they should be played with your second finger on the root, and fingers three and four on the middle strings. This might feel odd at first, but it frees up the first finger with which we'll add embellishments later.

Play through these G Major chords using the above fingering.

Example 1a

All of these shapes express the *sound* of G Major, so when we see several bars of G Major on a lead sheet, we can comp using different combinations of the shapes to provide movement. Although technically they are distinct, individual chords, they all fit with the harmony because they only use notes from the G Major scale.

Example 1b shows a simple rhythm pattern using these shapes. I've left off the chord names in this example because I want you to focus for on the G Major "sound" they make.

You should recognize that it sounds a bit like playing a walking bassline in G Major, only executed with chords, not single notes.

Example 1b

```
T|--4----4----5----5--|--7----7----5----7--|--9----9----7----7--|--9----7----5----4--|
A|--4----4----5----5--|--7----7----5----7--|--9----9----7----7--|--9----7----5----4--|
B|--3----3----5----5--|--7----7----5----7--|--8----8----7----7--|--8----7----5----3--|
```

Let's go a step further and begin to embellish these shapes using other notes of the G Major scale. The following exercises show how to do this. These aren't sophisticated comping chord phrases yet, but they will help to train your fingers and show you the possibilities of this style of playing.

Example 1c shows how moving just one note on the D string in each shape can create a simple harmonic movement. Suddenly, what could have been four bars of chugging on a single G Major chord has some direction and interest.

Use fingers 2, 3 and 4 to hold down the chords and to add the embellishment notes with the first finger.

Example 1c

Gmaj7   Am   Bm   Cmaj7   D7   Em   F#m   Gmaj7

let ring

```
T|--4-------5------|--7------9------|--11------12------|--14------16--|
A|--4----2--5----4-|--7---5--9----7-|--10---9--12---10-|--14---12-16--|
B|--3-------5------|--7------8------|--10------12------|--14------15--|
```

We can add movement to *any* of the three notes in these shapes. The following example adds movement on the G string.

Example 1d

To make things more musical, we can add notes from the G Major scale *above* and *below* the chord shapes. Play through Example 1e. Now the progression is beginning to sound less like an exercise and more like an etude.

Example 1e

We are only scratching the surface here. The previous examples have shown a few possible movements, but so far, we've only used three-note chords with a root on the low E string.

We can arrange these shapes on other string sets to open up new variations of this idea. The following set of grids show the harmonized G Major chords arranged on the D, G and B strings.

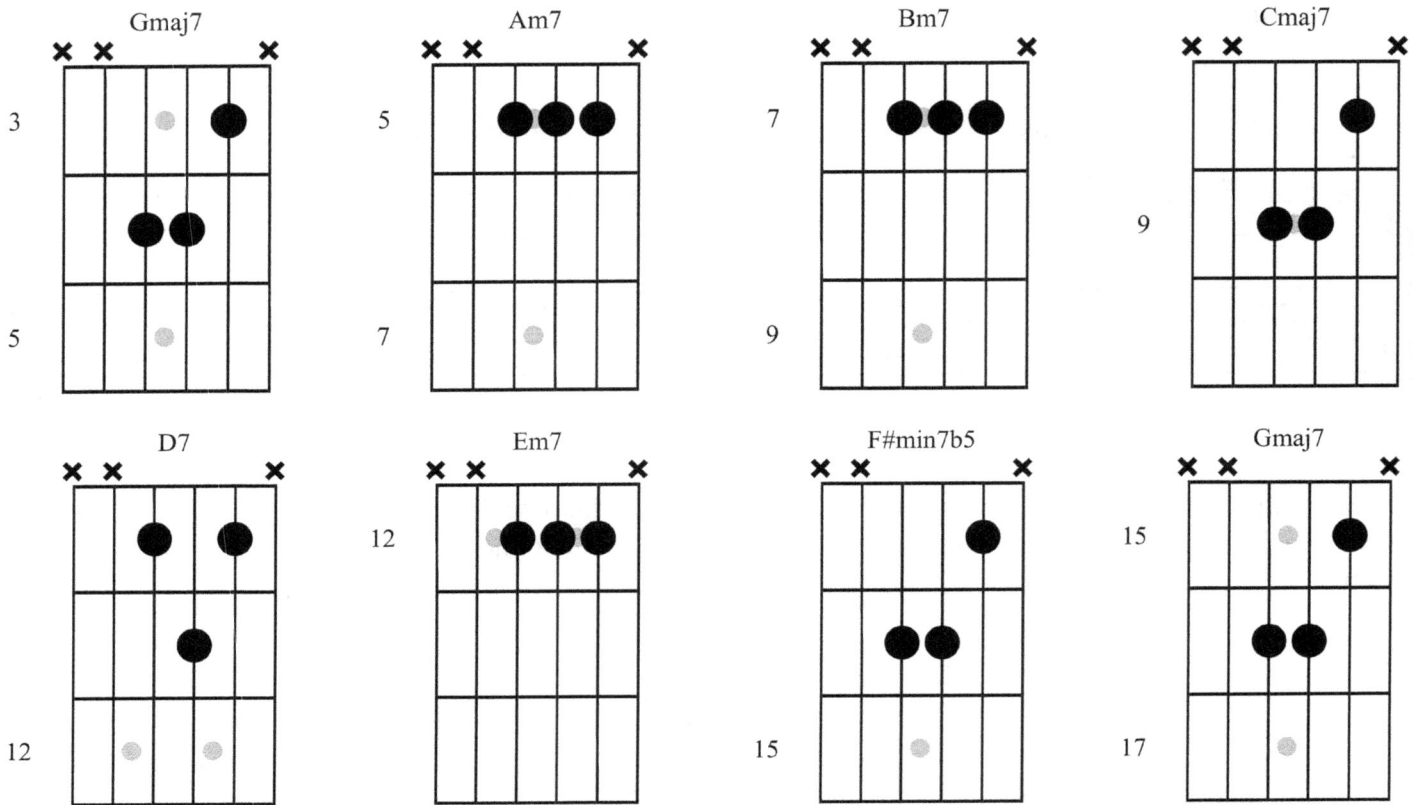

We can use this new set of shapes in the same way as before and add embellishments using the G Major scale. Here's an example chord phrase that uses notes a scale step above each chord tone on the B string.

Example 1f

At this point, let me introduce a new idea…

You *don't always* have to use scale tones to embellish a chord phrase – you can use chromatic/passing notes too (i.e. notes that don't belong to the parent scale).

A chromatic passing note is one from outside the key that leads somewhere, normally to another chord or scale tone. In jazz, chord/scale tones are often played on the strong downbeat and passing notes on the offbeat.

Here's a chord phrase that adds a scale tone above and a half step below each chord tone on the B string. In bars 1-3, the notes that are a half step below are all passing notes that don't belong to the G Major scale.

Despite this, we can still hear the *sound* of G Major because the passing notes quickly resolve to a chord tone. Listen to how this idea sounds.

Example 1g

So far, we've played these shapes in the order they appear in the harmonized scale sequence, but as you become more comfortable using them, you can mix things up to create less predictable chord phrases. Here are some examples.

Example 1h

Example 1i

This phrase draws on both sets of chord shapes.

Example 1j

The potential for creating comping phrases with this idea is vast. So far, we've created sixteen simple three-note voicings that we can use to play comping phrases over several bars of Gmaj7. However, we could also arrange these voicings on the high strings to create another eight options.

Also, the entire process can be repeated for minor chords and dominant chords. If you are prepared to put in the work, pursuing this idea means you'll have endless ways of connecting together chords in meaningful sequences. The only limit is your imagination. To practice this idea:

- Play through the harmonized chord shapes above until they become second nature to you, and you can easily switch between them

- Work out the G Major shapes on the G, B and high E string set and invent a few chord phrases of your own

- Listen to as much music as you can from the master jazz guitarists. The more music you absorb, the more you'll begin to hear these ideas in your head

Another way to harmonize G Major

I want to show you a useful variation of the above idea that John uses frequently in his playing.

It's based on the same principle, but now we will harmonize the G Major scale in four-note shapes. However, we'll be ignoring the 7th and using the root, 3rd, 5th, and **6th** intervals.

The 6th is a useful sound in jazz guitar comping, because it usually creates a stable sound over the harmony and the chords are easy to arrange across string sets.

To harmonize the G Major scale into 6ths chords, we build the four-note structure on each chord.

The first chord, G6, is formed with the notes G (root), B (3rd), D (5th) and E (6th).

To build the next chord in the sequence, begin on the A note and treat it as a *root* note (i.e. the I chord). To this we add C (3rd), E (5th) and F# (6th) notes to form an Am6 chord.

Now, move onto the B note and treat it as a root, etc.

The table below shows the full G Major scale harmonized into 6th chords.

Scale tone	G	A	B	C	D	E	F#
Chord	G6	Am6	Bmb6	C6	D6	Emb6	F#dim(b6)
	G B D E	A C E F#	B D F# G	C E G A	D F# A B	E G B C	F# A C D

There are two useful sets of shapes we can use to play these '6' chords. The first has root notes on the low E string and you would use these voicings when you want to comp a four-to-the-bar rhythm with a full sound with some movement and harmonic interest.

Play through them in sequence and listen to how they sound.

Here one example of how you can use these shapes to comp over several bars of G Major.

Example 1k

We can transfer these shapes onto other string sets. This time let's arrange them so that the root notes are located on the high E string. Note that the chord shapes are essentially the same as the previous set, we've just relocated the root from the low E to high E string.

This relatively simple idea has opened up a new range of options for creating comping patterns. We have chord shapes that we can play across the range of the neck, and we can also add embellishment notes to them.

16

Here are a few examples of how you can apply them.

Example 1l

Example 1m

Example 1n

Playing chord voicings across the fretboard

We've looked at various ways to embellish a single chord using its parent scale as a source, but this is not the only tool jazz guitarists use when comping. It's also useful to expand our chord knowledge, so that we can play inversions of the same chord anywhere on the neck.

When a pianist looks at the keyboard, they don't see chords as fixed positions that are played the same way every time. Rather, a chord is a just a series of notes spanning the entire keyboard in a linear fashion and can be accessed in many ways. Guitar players don't often view the fretboard in the same way but the results can be spectacular when they do.

When John was learning to play, his teacher, Chuck Wayne, had developed a more pianistic approach to playing the guitar that was especially tailored toward playing jazz. Below is a brief overview of his system, which is a great way to generate chord voicings all over the fretboard.

The thinking behind this system is that when we transpose a chord "shape" to another key, it doesn't always have the same *sonority*. In other words, it resonates differently because of the physical construction of the guitar.

Some voicings sound great in certain keys, but not in others. This system, however, is based on pianistic-style voicings on guitar that have the same sonorous quality, regardless of the key. All the chord voicings are four-note forms, so each one chord can be expressed four ways (as inversions with each note as the lowest).

There are several ways of arranging these chords:

- On adjacent strings

- With the lowest note on one string, skipping a string, then arranging the three upper notes on adjacent strings

- With the two lowest notes on adjacent strings, then skipping a string, then the two highest notes on adjacent strings

This method is great for generating many ways to play one chord in all areas of the neck.

Below I have illustrated the <ref> "open voicings" (all the notes are on adjacent strings) of Cmaj7, organized into *lower*, *mid* and *high*.

You can see that this method creates 12 different ways to play Cmaj7, and we're only using *one* of the three construction methods.

Cmaj7 has the notes C (root), E (3rd), G (5th) and B (7th)

The voicings below use only these four notes and no note is duplicated. The chords are arranged from low to high on the neck, so that you can play them in sequence.

The tricky stretch required to play Cmaj7/E in the mid set is easier if you barre your first finger at the 5th fret.

Chuck Wayne style four-note voicings

Lower set

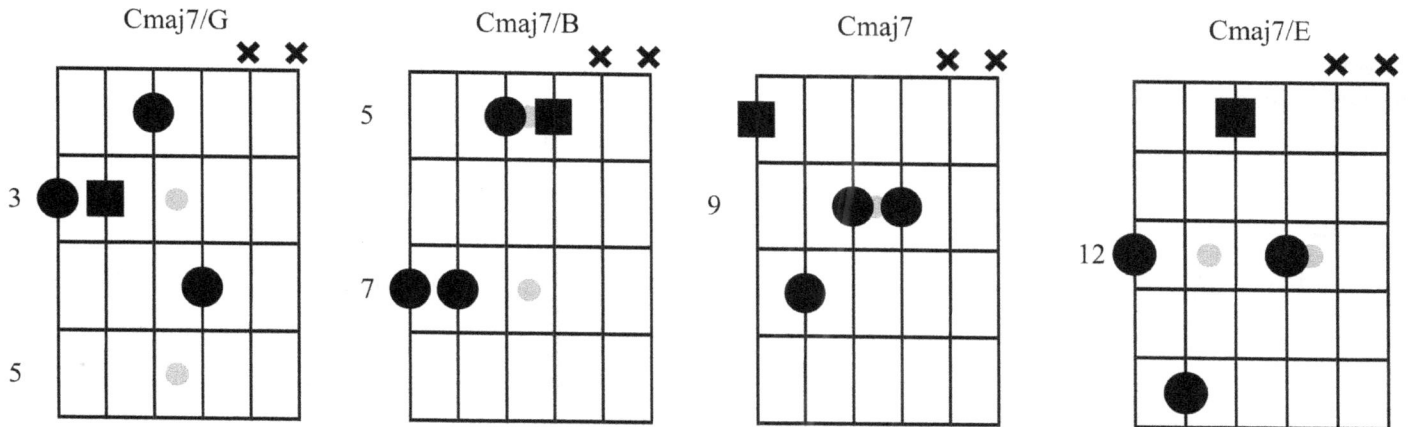

Mid set

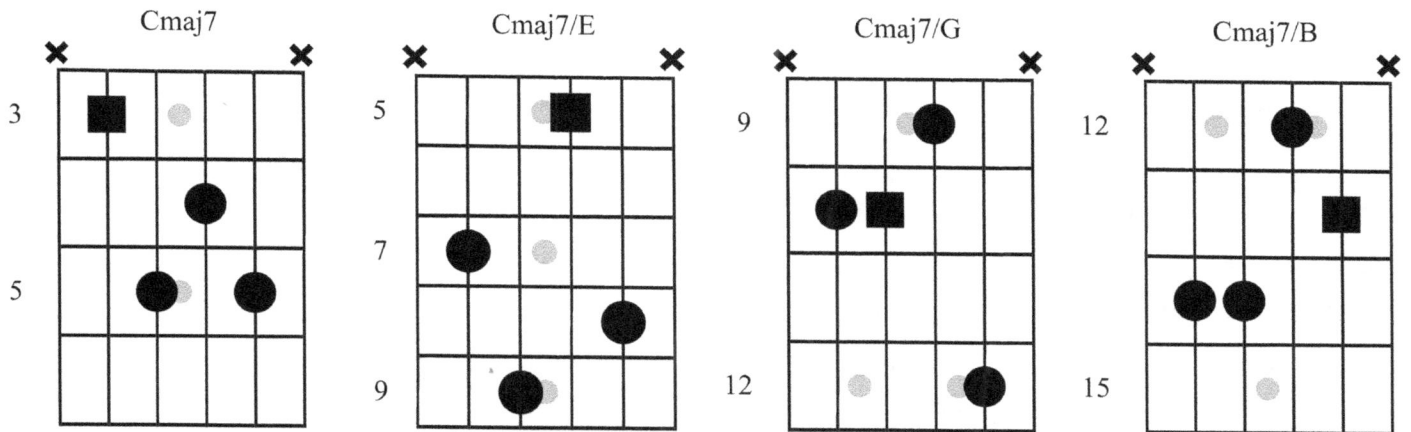

High set

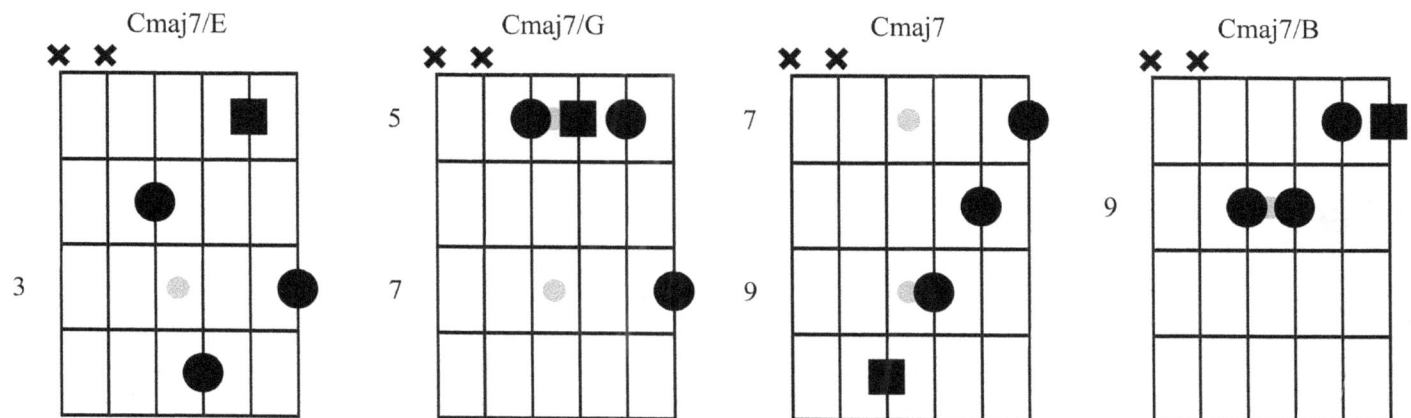

This is just one way of generating chord voicings across the neck. There are, of course, other well-established systems and it's always good to explore different approaches, but this system was conceived by a jazz guitarist with other guitar players in mind.

Your long-term goal should be to combine the ideas of embellishing chords with movement, and using many voicings of the same chord, to create comping phrases.

Fundamental Changes publish some great resources that will help with this task, including **Jazz Guitar Chord Mastery** and **Jazz Guitar Chord Creativity**.

Diminished connecting chords

To end this chapter, I want to give you one more tool you can use when creating comping lines. You'll see that this idea crops up frequently in John's playing.

We've seen that it's possible to generate many inversions of chords to navigate the fretboard, but sometimes we still need a way of connecting chords to fill a gap between voicings. One useful tool to do this is the diminished/half-diminished chord.

Diminished chords have a dissonant sound that strongly wants to resolve to a "home" chord. We can use this characteristic to our advantage when comping.

Take the following simple progression:

Fmaj7 – Gm – Fmaj7 – Dm7

This progression doesn't have much movement or harmonic interest, but we can use diminished shapes as connecting chords to create movement between the original chords.

In bar one of Example 1o, an F#dim7 chord connects Fmaj7 and Gm7. As well as filling the gap, it creates an ascending chromatic bass note movement.

At the end of bar one, we can continue the chromatic bass ascent and use a G#dim7 to approach the F chord (voiced with its 3rd in the bass). Similarly, the Dm7 chord in bar three can be approached from a half-step below by C#dim7.

With the addition of some passing single notes, a potentially quite boring sequence now has movement and direction.

Example 1o

Now here's a way to use inversions of a diminished chord connect chords. An inversion of a chord simply means that you play the same selection of notes with a different bass note. Diminished chords can be moved around the fretboard and *invert* themselves simply by shifting the same shape up in minor third intervals (a distance of three frets).

This means that C#dim7, Edim7, Gdim7 and A#dim7 and are all inversions of each other – they all contain the same notes but have a different bass note.

The original chord progression below might simply have read Gm7 – Dm7, but this example uses the idea that C#dim7 wants to resolve to Dm7 and adds inversions of C#dim7 to move between Gm7 and Dm7.

Listen to how this idea sounds.

Example 1p

| Gm7 | Gm9 | Gdim7 | C#dim7 | Dm7 | Edim7 | Dm7 |

```
e|-------------------------------------------------------------------|
B|-------5-------3-------5-------6-------8-------10-------------------|
G|-------5-------2-------3-------5-------6-------10-------------------|
D|-3-----5-------3-------5-------7-------8-------10-------------------|
A|-3-------------2-------4-------5-------7-------10-------------------|
E|-3-----------------------------------------------------------------|
```

Just as we built chord shapes on the notes of the major scale earlier, we can do the same on any minor scale. Plus, we can add some diminished shapes into the mix. If I saw two bars of a static F minor chord on a lead sheet, for instance, I might play something like this:

Example 1q

| Fm | Gdim | Ab6 | Bbdim | Cm11(b6) | Dbdim | Edim | Fm |

```
e|-1-----3-----4-----6-----8-----9-----12-----13-----|
B|-1-----2-----4-----5-----6-----8-----11-----13-----|
G|-1-----3-----5-----6-----8-----9-----12-----13-----|
D|-3-----2-----3-----5-----6-----8-----11-----10-----|
```

Here, I used the notes of the F Harmonic Minor scale on the high E string and built a chord voicing on each scale tone. This type of idea can be used over long bars of a single chord, or on modal jazz tunes (such as over the four bars of Fm7 that open Herbie Hancock's *Cantaloupe Island*).

Space won't allow a more in-depth exploration of this idea here, but keep in mind the principle that you can use a diminished/half-diminished chord in the same way you might use an approach note when playing a bebop solo line. They always want to resolve to a target.

There are many ideas in this chapter that warrant deeper investigation.

We've explored some of the theory and principles of how to embellish chords to create comping patterns.

We've also looked at a method for opening up the fretboard and thinking in a more pianistic way about chord voicings.

Aim to work through some of these ideas in your practice sessions but don't get too bogged down in the theory. In the chapters that follow, we take a practical look at the ideas John plays, and he wants you to simply absorb the ones you like into your musical vocabulary and use them in your comping. You can figure out why they work later.

The following examples show the greatest chord phrases from a master comper and are based on some of the most common chord sequences in jazz. You'll also learn John's approach to playing some of the all-time great jazz standards, and you can use these as study pieces for your practice times.

Treat this book like a phrase book and learn to speak the language of jazz guitar comping.

Enjoy!

Chapter Two: Major ii V I Movements

In this chapter I want to show you some of my favorite moves on the most common chord sequence in jazz – the Major ii V I.

The Major ii V I cadence features in virtually every tune of the jazz repertoire, and if you learn many ways to navigate it you'll have vocabulary for any jazz standard you might want to play.

The first few examples are in the key of C Major, so the underlying progression they relate to is:

Dm7 (ii) – G7 (V) Cmaj7 (I)

This particular ii V I occurs frequently in *Fly Me To The Moon*. Later, in Chapter Three, you'll learn a full comping arrangement of that tune, but first let's do a ii V I workout and explore some creative options you can use on this essential sequence.

In jazz, many jazz players view the ii and V chords as performing the same function – in fact, you can view the ii chord as simply "unraveling" into the V. Both chords function as a way to lead the harmony to the home chord (chord I). Of course, the strongest sound of the ii V I progression is the movement from V to the I. In one sense, the ii simply exists to prepare the V and is actually often ignored.

As dominant chords can be easily altered or extended, the ii chord is often replaced by a rich sounding variation of the V chord.

In Example 2a, the ii chord (Dm7) is omitted and replaced with an extended G7 (G13) that moves to the original altered V chord in bar two before resolving to the I chord (Cmaj7) in bar three.

Example 2a

Or, the V to I movement could be played like this, with a little more movement added and more colorful voicings.

Example 2b

Instead of adding variation to the V chord, it's also possible to focus on embellishing the ii chord. Either approach is valid, because the ii and V produce a similar sound.

The idea behind Example 2c is to play many small voicings around a D minor tonal center before moving to G7. You'll see that I've taken a few harmonic liberties with this idea.

In bar one, I used a diminished connecting chord and added a chromatic approach chord (Dbm7) from a half step below to create an extra step in the sequence.

You'll also notice the small dominant chord voicing of D7sus4. Although technically correctly named here, I'm really just embellishing a regular Dm7 chord. Hold down the Dm7 chord shape at the 5th fret, then play the note on the B string 8th fret with your pinkie. You'll be in position to play the Dm7 shape that follows.

In bar three, the G7#9 chord produces a tense sound that increases the pull towards the resolution of Cmaj7.

Example 2c

Often, my chord phrases are built on melodic lines that I invent and when I play a chord phrase, I'll usually have a simple melody in mind. The job is then to build chord voicings beneath this melody that keep the melody on top. However, this is where the hard work of Chapter One pays off and you'll see those approaches all in use here to help me access the melody notes I need.

Compare the first two bars of examples 2c and 2d and play the top line melody of each on the high strings. You'll hear that the melody is almost identical but in example 2d I've used different chords to harmonize it. You'll hear that the two ideas create a completely different effect.

Example 2d

To work on developing your own similar ideas, try writing a melody over a ii V I in C Major, allowing one bar for each chord. Play the melody notes only on the B and high E strings.

First, try to harmonize those notes into small chord shapes. Refer back to the Chuck Wayne C Major voicings if you get stuck and try to find some chord voicings you like the sound of.

Next, work on finding several chord voicings for each chord in the progression.

Now combine these two ideas and see if you can create some chord phrase movements that complement the melody you invented.

Tip: don't make the melody too complex to begin with, keep it simple!

For the next two examples we switch to play a ii V I (Am7 D7 GMaj7) in the key of G Major.

In Example 2e, first play the top note of every voicing in the progression to hear the melody I had in mind.

Now play through the chords in bar one and notice how the movement is created. The main chord sound is A minor. The notes on the G and B strings remain the same throughout the bar. While the notes on the high E string take care of the melody, the notes on the D string descend chromatically.

Remember that the underlying progression is Am7 – D7 – Gmaj7, now take a look at bar two and see how I've interpreted the D7 section.

Given the melody note on the B string, I could have played a standard "Hendrix chord" D7#9 shape, but I wanted something more colorful, so opted for this unusual D7#5#9 chord, voiced with its C note in the bass.

The Ab dominant chords that follow are b5 substitutions for D7 (Ab is a b5 or tritone interval away from D7). This is a common movement and chromatically it leads perfectly to G major (another unusual voicing, this time a Gmaj13).

Example 2e

Sometimes, my comping is more about creating movement in the bass than building chords around a top line melody.

In Example 2f I wanted to create a strong descending bassline that gravitates toward the I chord (Gmaj7). I've changed up the progression quite a bit here. First, I've "compressed" the ii – V chord movement into one bar and shifted it into bar two. I'm using bar one to approach the Am7 chord chromatically from above. Although this is quite a departure from the original Am7 – D7 – Gmaj7, you can hear the overall intention of the chord phrase – it's all heading toward Gmaj7.

Example 2f

If you find a chord movement you really like, experiment by transposing it to other keys. Each key has its own sonority, and some ideas will convert better than others, depending on the chord voicings used. We can also use the uniqueness of each key to our advantage and discover neat movements we can play that are specific to that key.

For the remaining few examples in this chapter we'll change key to the key of F Major with the ii V I chords being Gm7 C7 and FMaj7.

To begin with, here's a minimalist ii V I movement. This is the type of line you should experiment with to create your own ideas. We have voicings that are close together and we can use simple single notes to connect them to make a meaningful phrase.

Example 2g

Here's a line which is trickier to play than it appears on paper and uses ascending notes from the F Major scale to form the melodic line. It's played in 3/4 time, but the 1/8th notes in bar one are played straight.

Listen to the audio to hear this example and you'll get the idea.

Example 2h

Next, here's another chord phrase driven by a top line melody. This chordal idea has a Bossa Nova feel and is the kind of thing I might play over the ii V I segment of *The Girl from Ipanema*.

Example 2i

Here is a more complex idea built around a top line melody. It's typical of the kind of line I'd play if I wanted something more decorative over *The Girl from Ipanema*.

Example 2j

Here's another ascending line idea you can use over the same chord sequence.

Example 2k

Here's a similar ascending idea, but this time with every note harmonized. The idea this time was to use many voicings of the ii chord and ignore the V chord until just before the I chord.

Example 2l

In this final Major ii V I example I begin the chord phrase with a D7 sound in the pickup bar, functions as a V chord, leading to G minor. This line also includes a diminished connecting chord to harmonize one of the melody notes.

Example 2m

I hope this chapter has shown you that it's possible to turn a routine sounding ii V I into a much more interesting chord phrase.

In the next chapter we are going to put many of these Major ii V I ideas to work in a study piece of the well-known standard *Fly Me to the Moon*.

Chapter Three: Study Piece (based on *Fly Me to the Moon*)

When you learn new ideas it's important to play them in the context of real music right away. When you apply them to a tune you know well, it makes it much easier to embed the ideas and make them a natural part of your comping vocabulary.

In this chapter, I've improvised a chorus of the tune *Fly Me to the Moon* and in it you'll find examples of all the comping devices we've discussed, along with a few others:

- Melody-led lines harmonized into chord voicings

- Bassline-led chord movements

- Many voicings per chord

- Some changes to the quality of chords (dominant 7 instead of minor 7)

- Plus, some b5 chord substitution ideas

I'll highlight certain sections of this arrangement to explain my thinking behind the chord phrases. When you play the full arrangement, be sure to slow things right down at first and get all the chord shapes under your fingers before speeding things up. This way you'll lock the fretting hand movements into muscle memory, allowing you to concentrate on playing smoothly and making the lines swing. Listen to the audio download to hear exactly how I play it.

Overview of the basic chords

It's easy to take a jazz arrangement at face value and play it without really understanding the harmonic choices the composer made when putting it together. An understanding of the basic chord changes of the tune helps us to see:

- Where chords have been extended or altered

- Where the quality of chords has been changed (e.g. minor 7 chords turned into dominant 7s)

- Where chord substitution ideas have been used

- Where additional chord changes have been added to enrich the harmony for soloists (e.g. adding ii chords before V chords)

With that in mind, here are the basic changes for *Fly Me to the Moon* and are the chords commonly played by most jazz musicians. The original "piano roll" sheet music may differ a little, as certain alterations to the changes have become embedded over time.

The tune has a simple AB form and many of the chord changes are repeated.

The A section is as follows:

| Am7 | Dm7 | G7 | Cmaj7 |

| Fmaj7 | Bm7b5 | E7b9 | Am7 A7 |

| Dm7 | G7 | Cmaj7 F7 | Em7 A7 |

And here are the B section chords:

| Am7 | Dm7 | G7 | Cmaj7 |

| Fmaj7 | Bm7b5 | E7b9 | Am7 A7 |

| Dm7 | G7 | Em7 | A7 |

| Dm7 | G7 | Cmaj7 | Bm7b5 E7b9 |

Now let's look at some specific points of interest in the arrangement.

Example 3a focuses on bars 9-12 of the arrangement.

The various D minor voicings in bar nine are a smooth way to quickly shift from the fifth to tenth position. In bar ten, the three-note chord looks like an F diminished triad but is actually a G7b9 without the root note. In bar eleven, the chromatic passing note on the B string 7th fret is the #11 of Cmaj7, but is really just a passing note targeting the 5th of the chord on the 8th fret.

Example 3a

Example 3b focuses on bars 17-21 and features a favorite Latin jazz lick of mine. A great way of creating movement on a static minor chord is to hold the basic chord shape and add moving lines within it by altering notes – just as we did for the Gmaj7 chord in Chapter One.

Here, in the first two bars, the moving notes on the D string suggest that the chords move between straight minor 7ths and minor-major 7ths.

In bars 20-21, the movement from C7 to Fmaj7 is played with an ascending chromatic bassline using 10th chord voicings. (A 10th chord is just a simple root plus 3rd voicing, with the 3rd pushed up an octave).

Example 3b

Finally, Example 3c (bars 25-28 of the arrangement), features an ascending idea that covers a wide range of the neck via a series of predominantly closed voicings. Notice that I included a connecting C#dim chord to fill the space between D minor voicings.

Example 3c

Now here's the full arrangement. First have a listen to the audio recording, then work your way through it a few bars at a time.

Example 3d – Based on the changes of *Fly Me to the Moon*

Dm/C
C♯ dim
G13
D♭9
C6add9
B7sus4♭5
E7♯9
Am7
AmMaj7
Am7
Dm
DmMaj7
Dm7
Dm69
Fdim
Cmaj7
C7
Fmaj7
F6
Bm7
E7♯9
Am7
A7
Dm7
A♯dim
Dm/C
Dm69
Cmaj7
B♭7

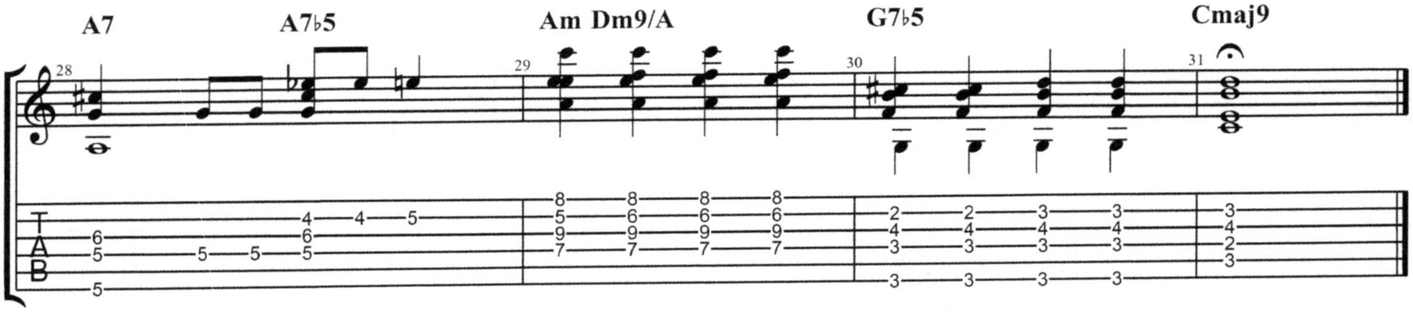
A7
A7♭5
Am Dm9/A
G7♭5
Cmaj9
TAB

Chapter Four: I VI ii V Movements

Another common major key sequence in jazz is the I vi ii V progression. You'll recognize this sound immediately as a turnaround – i.e. the chords at the end of a tune that "turn it around" to begin again. It's the main feature of all Rhythm Changes tunes (songs based on the changes to the original *I Got Rhythm* by George Gershwin).

Most of the examples in this chapter are in G Major, and in this key the I vi ii V sequence is:

Gmaj7 (I) – Em7 (vi) – Am7 (ii) – D7 (V)

However, it's common to change the quality of chord vi to a dominant 7 (E7), so look out for this in the lines that follow.

It's also common to add chord substitution ideas to this progression. If you play it as written above, you'll notice that it just loops around in a circle and the harmonic movement is quite limited. Em7 has a lot of notes in common with Gmaj7, and the ii chord Am7 serves a similar purpose to the V chord D7 in wanting to resolve back to Gmaj7 as we discussed in the previous chapter.

To make things more interesting, certain substitutions are often introduced, such as replacing chord I with chord iii. For example, the I vi ii V…

Gmaj7 – Em7 – Am7 – D7

Becomes iii VI ii V

Bm7 – E7 – Am7 – D7

This progression also lends itself well to b5 substitutions on the dominant chords. So,

Gmaj7 – Em7 – Am7 – D7

Becomes…

Gmaj7 – E7 – Eb7 – D7 (Eb7 is the b5 of Am7)

Or,

Gmaj7 – E7 – Am7 – Ab7 (Ab7 is the b5 of D7)

Or,

Bm11 – Bb7b5 – Am11 – Ab7b5

This last idea includes b5 substitutions for both the E7 and D7. Bb7b5 is the b5 of E7, and Ab7b5 is the b5 of D7; plus, this version includes the chord iii for chord I substitution).

All these ideas feature in the lines that follow.

In bar two of Example 4a, I've included both an extended/altered V chord and its dominant b5 substitution. For the V chord, we need to play a rootless voicing of D13(b9) in this position, as the D bass note is not accessible.

This chord is more usually played using the shape below. It's generally used when we want to add even more tension before resolving to the I chord.

D13(b9)

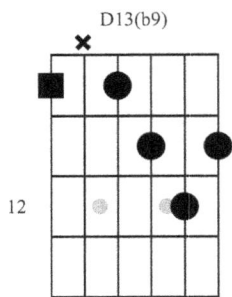

This is followed by the equally tense sounding Ab7b5, the b5 substitution of D7, which leads chromatically to Gmaj7.

Example 4a

Example 4b is a variation on the previous line with more decoration.

In bar one there is a chromatic Fm7 chord which is used to approach the Em7 from a half step above, and in bar two, some additional chord movement and passing notes.

This idea illustrates the fact that once you have the basic chord shape movements under your fingers, you can embellish them in endless different ways.

Example 4b

The next example begins in a similar way to Example 4b, but the Em7 is a rootless voicing. I then embellish the A minor chord differently in bar two.

You'll notice that I often use this 7sus4 voicing as a passing chord, and it works especially well when paired with a minor 9 voicing.

Example 4c

As you learned in Chapter One, comping can include chord movements, walking basslines and single note lines. These are all tools in our armory, we just need to apply them with taste and discretion.

This next example includes two ideas you can use to freshen up your comping moves.

The first is to use chords/bassline movements to approach a target chord. In bar one, I ignore the VI chord (E7) and focus on the ii chord (Am7) which is approached chromatically from a whole step above.

The second idea is to outline the harmony with single note lines.

Playing what is essentially a lead line is fine when playing solo guitar, but it can also work well when comping for others as long as we use our ears. It can be effective, for example, when backing a singer and to provide a line in counterpoint to the melody.

Interspersing chordal passages with single lines can also create space and contrast in an arrangement, so do experiment with this idea.

Example 4d

In the next example I use voicings for the chords that keep them as close together as possible, only requiring one or two notes to change to spell out the following chord.

The choice of the G6 shape on the top four strings puts me in the right area of the neck to access the E9. From there, rather than play a straight A minor chord, I opted for a more colorful Am9b5, which has a bittersweet sound to it. Play this line with plenty of swing!

Example 4e

Here's another approach for you to consider. If you build a comping passage by starting with a melody line, you have the choice whether to harmonize every note, or just some of the notes. I'll often play lines like the one in bar two, where I just punctuate the line with chords, but equally I could have played a voicing on every note.

At the end of this idea I wanted to keep the G bass note sounding and play descending notes on the D string. Above the notation I've written in the chord sound that each note suggests over the G bass.

Example 4f

The next example begins with the common substitution idea of replacing chord I with chord iii (Bm7 in place of GMaj7). This is often done to create variety within a repeating I vi ii V pattern. It avoids the repetition of the I chord, but also suggests different melodic possibilities to soloists. As with most chord substitution ideas, it works on the basis of the two chords sharing common notes:

Gmaj7 = G, B, D, F#

Bm7 = B, D, F#, A

In this example the B minor chord is followed by some E7 variations that include many altered notes. If someone told you to play a Dm7b5 chord, you'd probably automatically reach for this shape in fifth position but used in a different context over an E bass note, you actually create an E7#5b9.

In bar three, the progression ends on Bm11, rather than Gmaj7. It's the chord iii for chord I substitution again. If you happen to be working with a bassist who is playing the G root note at this point, the harmony will still work. Bm11 over a G bass note creates the effect of a G6/9 chord.

Example 4g

A simple way to really make your lines swing is to play occasional 1/8th note triplets over a straight-ahead groove. This effect creates the feeling of pushing/pulling against the beat that characterizes jazz swing. The more smoothly you can play it, the hipper your comping will sound. Listen to the audio to nail the timing and don't rush the triplets.

Example 4h

In Chapter One, we looked at the idea of using the harmonized chords of the G Major scale to provide movement in our comping patterns. Here's that idea put to use.

In bar one, after playing the Gadd9 chord, I had E7#5b9 in mind as my target chord. To get there, I used Am7 and Bm7 chords, with a chromatic Bbm7 in between.

A common way to target a dominant 7 chord is by playing its ii chord (Bm7 is the ii chord of E7) and you'll see this idea crop up frequently in jazz standards. Look at the chord changes of Charlie Parker's classic *Blues for Alice*, and you'll see that it's a basic blues progression that has been enhanced with many additional ii V movements including chromatic ii Vs. Each movement leads to a *destination* chord.

Example 4i

The final example is based on the opening chords of *Embraceable You,* which we'll study in the next chapter. This may not appear to be a I vi ii V at first glance, but actually it is – just a well-disguised one!

The Bbdim chord in bar one is a b5 substitution for E7. In bar four, Bm7 is a substitution for D7 (the chords have three out of four notes in common) and on guitar it works well to move between two minor chord a whole step apart to create a riff or chord phrase (Am7 to Bm7).

The function of the E7 chord at the end of bar four is different from earlier. Here it's functioning as the V chord leading to A minor, rather than being the VI chord in G Major.

Example 4j

Chapter Five: Study Piece (based on *Embraceable You*)

Embraceable You is a timeless Gershwin tune. It was written in 1928 and first published two years later when it appeared in the Broadway musical *Girl Crazy*. It was performed by Ginger Rogers in her debut as a Broadway leading lady. The orchestra for the performance included legendary musicians Benny Goodman, Glenn Miller, Jack Teagarden, Jimmy Dorsey and Gene Krupa. Gershwin himself conducted the band at its premier, and they held jam sessions during each intermission!

All the jazz greats have recorded this tune which is most often thought of as a bittersweet ballad, but as with all jazz standards there have been many different versions from fast to slow to Latin! This arrangement was recorded at 70bpm.

One of Gershwin's trademarks as a composer was his approach of repeating melodic phrases while varying the harmony underneath to create a completely different sound and you can hear that device at work in this tune.

Overview of the basic chords

First, let's look at the commonly played chord changes to *Embraceable You*. It has an ABAC structure, as follows:

A section:

| Gmaj7 | Bb°7 | Am7 | D7 |

| Am7 | Cm6 | Gmaj7 | F#m7b5 B7b9 |

B section:

| Em Em/D | C#m7b5 F#7b5 | Bm7 | Em7 A7 |

| Dmaj7 Bm7 | Em7 A7 | Am7 | D7 |

A section repeats, which a slight variation in the last bar:

| Gmaj7 | Bb°7 | Am7 | D7 |

| Am7 | Cm6 | Gmaj7 | Dm7 G7 |

C section:

| Cmaj7 | F#m7b5 B7b9 | Em7 Emaj7/D | C#m7b5 Cm6 |

| Bm7 E7 | Am7b5 D7b9 | Gmaj7 | Am7 D7 |

Before we get to the arrangement, let me highlight a few of the comping ideas I used.

Example 5a shows the line used in bars 15-17.

To play the descending triplet phrase in bar fifteen, bar your first finger at the 5th fret and keep it in place while playing the high notes using your fourth finger.

Use the same approach to play the A minor chord phrase that follows in bar sixteen.

Example 5a

Example 5b is bars 17-20 of the arrangement.

In bars 17-18, be careful to execute the ascending chromatic lines cleanly while still retaining the swing feel – it's easy to allow these to sound a bit loose!

To create movement over the A minor chord in bars 19-20 I alternate it with C major and also use an augmented voicing to fill the gap and create a brief tension. The augmented chord idea occurred to me based purely on its proximity to the Am/D voicing I was already playing!

To play these moving voices, the easiest way is to hold down the chords with your first, second and third fingers, then fret the D bass note with your thumb. Then you'll need to quickly change the fretting hand back to its normal position to play the chromatic descending chords in bar twenty.

Example 5b

Now listen to the audio of the full arrangement a couple of times before attempting it.

It's a slightly more challenging piece to play than *Fly Me to the Moon* as it contains more moving lines and counterpoint ideas. To break it down, focus on any bars you find tricky to begin with and learn those slowly.

You'll find the whole thing easier to play if you understand that the majority of the time I'm holding down a common chord shape and playing melodic ideas around it, while *still holding* that shape – just like the A minor ideas in Example 5a.

If you see a line and think, *it's not possible to reach those notes while holding this chord shape*, then I've moved position!

But there is an internal logic to the arrangement and the series of chord shapes I'm holding. As Joe Pass once said, "Why would you want to play anything *difficult*?!"

Example 5c

Am7 Bm7 E13♭9 Am7 D7♯9 D7♭9
G B♭dim Am/D Eaug/D C/D Eaug/D
Bm7 B♭m Am Bm7 B♭m7 C Cmaj7 Cm6 E♭m69 Cm9
Gmaj7 Am B♭m Bm Am Gmaj7 A♭7add13 G7add13 G7(♯5)
Cmaj7 C6add9 F♯m11 B7♯5♭9 B7♯5 Em7 G/D

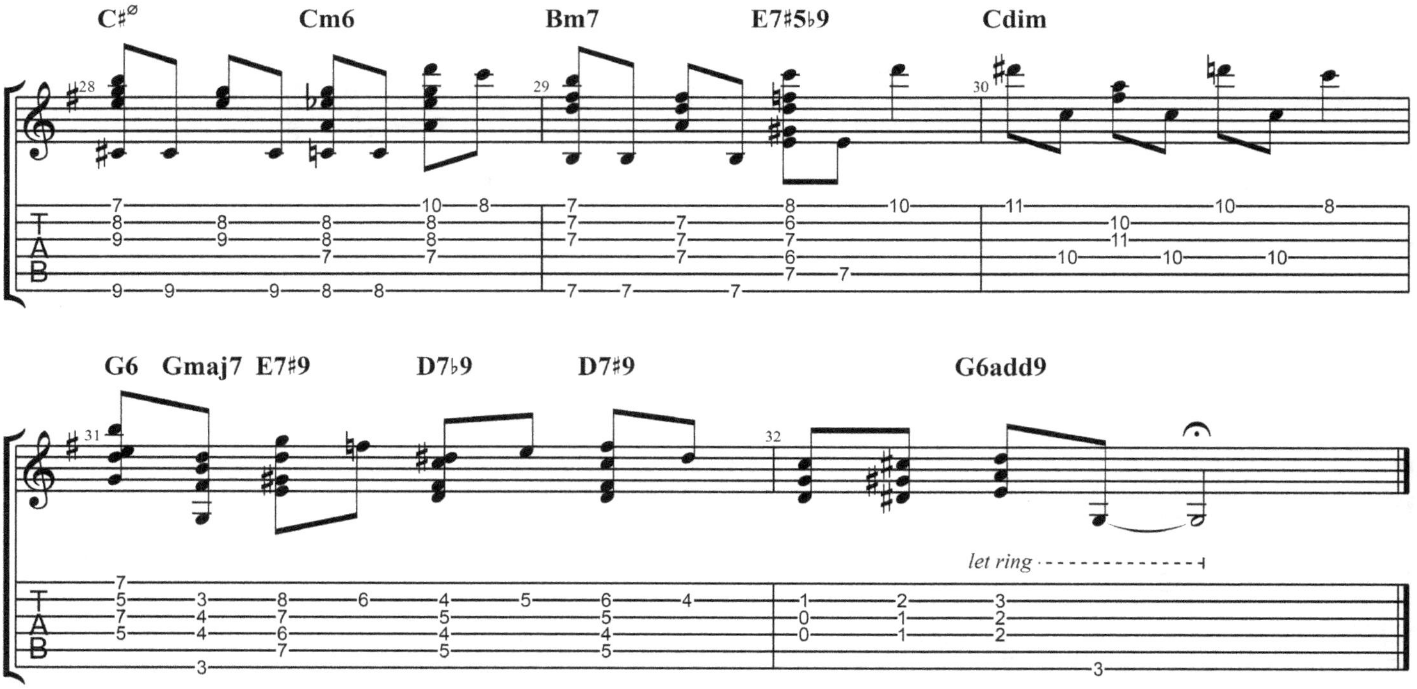
C♯ø
Cm6
Bm7
E7♯5♭9
Cdim
G6
Gmaj7
E7♯9
D7♭9
D7♯9
G6add9
let ring

Chapter Six: Study Piece (based on *Have You Met Miss Jones*)

Before we move on to look at the Minor ii V i progression, here is another study piece for you to work on. It's based on another tune that uses the major I VI ii V progression and contains lots of shifting major ii V I movements.

Have You Met Miss Jones? is a Rodgers and Hart tune, and the melody is so beautifully written that it disguises the complex harmonic ideas that support it. It has an AABA form, where the A section is a straightforward repeating I VI ii V progression, but the B section is more complex.

Here are the standard chord changes for the A section. Notice the chord iii for chord I substitution in bar four (Am7 in place of Fmaj7).

A section:

| Fmaj7 | D7 | Gm7 | C7 |

| Am7 | Dm7 | Gm7 | C7 |

This form repeats, and the second time around the last two bars change to Cm7 to F7, to set up the bridge or B section.

B section:

| Bbmaj7 | Abm7 Db7 | Gbmaj7 | Em7 A7 |

| Dmaj7 | Abm7 Db7 | Gbmaj7 | Gm7 C7 |

At first glance, it's hard to see how the shifting tonal centers of the B section relate to one another. It can also be a challenging set of changes to solo over, because the key changes fall in unusual places. So, what's happening here?

The B section is essentially based around "Coltrane changes" that were written before John Coltrane composed *Three Little* Words and later his famous *Giant Steps*. The core idea is based around tonal centers that move in major thirds (four frets on guitar) in either direction.

- The first key center of Bb Major shifts down a major third to Gb Major

- Gb Major shifts down a major third to D Major

- D Major shifts back up a major third to Gb Major

The cycle is broken by the Gm7 to C7 chord change which is there to help lead back to the key of F Major.

This leads back into the A section, which this time is slightly modified to have a definite ending.

| Fmaj7 Bb7 | Am7 D7 | Gm7 | C7 |

| Am7 D7 | Gm7 C7 | F6 | Gm7 C7 |

I play two comping versions of this tune that both offer different approaches.

The first is the simpler of the two arrangements and focuses on using simple chord forms connected by walking bassline movements.

When you first set out to comp through a standard tune, this is a good place to start. Don't try to come up with complex or clever ideas right away. Instead, map out the basic geography of the tune, noticing where the chord changes fall and what simple voicings you can use.

My good friend Ted Greene, who knew more than anyone about advanced, sophisticated chord voicings, still always said, "Focus on simple chords, melody and having good rhythm."

Once you know the geography of the changes, begin to connect them with bassline movements and focus on keeping good time and making it swing.

Once you have a solid, simple arrangement that moves through the basic changes, then you can begin to think about creating comping phrases that use more of the range of the guitar.

Try this first arrangement and work with a metronome set to a modest tempo. Only speed up when you can play it perfectly without making a mistake. Aim to reach around 120bpm via small increments.

Example 6a

A♭m7
D♭7
Gm7
C7
Fmaj7
Gm7
B♭/C
C13♭9
Fmaj9/C
Dm7
D♭m7
Cm7
B7♭5
B♭6
B♭
A♭m7
D♭7
G♭6
Dmaj7

The second arrangement is a more complex chordal workout that combines many of the ideas we've looked at so far, with many voicings for chords, chromatic approach chords, diminished connecting chords, and a couple of substitution ideas.

Once again, it's important to take this slowly to begin with. Commit all the shapes and movements to muscle memory and then focus on playing the chord stabs cleanly.

You can play an arrangement like this with a pick or with thumb and fingers, Wes Montgomery style. Try both and see which you prefer.

Example 6b

Em7/A
A∅
F7alt
B♭6/9
A♭m9
G♭maj9
Em7
A13
Dmaj9
A♭m7
G♭maj7
Gm9
C13
Fmaj9
B♭7♭5
Am7
D7♯9
Gm9
C13
C9

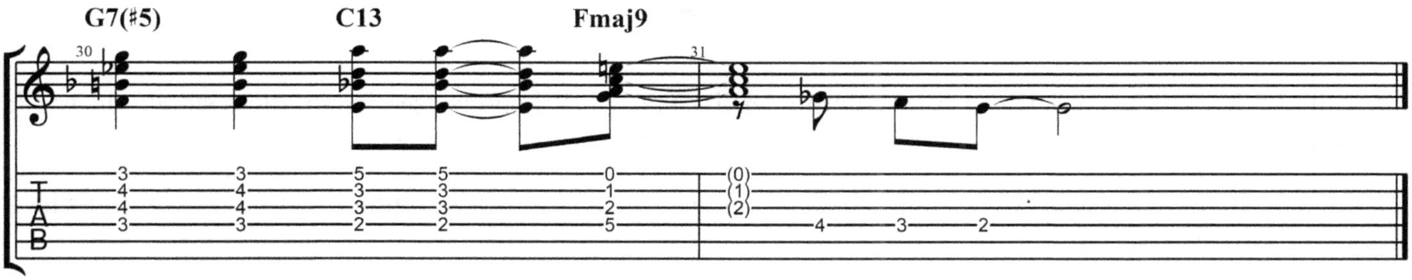
G7(#5)
C13
Fmaj9

Chapter Seven: Minor ii V I Movements

The Minor ii V i progression is nearly as common as the Major ii V I and is used in countless standards, so it's essential to have some chord vocabulary for it under your fingers.

First, it's useful to understand where this sequence comes from and how it's commonly used in jazz. Let's look at it in the key of A Minor.

The Minor ii V i progression is created by harmonizing the notes of the harmonic minor scale. The table below shows the notes of A Harmonic Minor and the chords it generates when the notes are stacked in thirds.

I	ii	III	iv	V	VI	VII
A	B	C	D	E	F	G#
Am(Maj7)	Bm7b5	Cmaj7#5	Dmin7	E7	Fmaj7	G#dim7

In the key of A Minor, the ii V i sequence is therefore Bm7b5 – E7 – Am(Maj7).

Strictly speaking, the I chord should be a minor-major 7, but this is rarely how it's played in a jazz setting. Over the years, it has become common practice to adjust the sound of this dissonant chord for Western ears and play it as a straight minor chord, so that it sounds less unresolved.

The same kind of latitude is applied to the ii chord, which may be played as any kind of straight or extended minor chord.

The V chord is usually played as an altered dominant 7 (often written just as E7alt), which means we get to decide what tensions to add to it.

With this in mind, let's look at some example chord phrases.

Example 7a uses a Bm11 in place of Bm7b5, an altered E7, then an Am6 in place of the minor-major 7.

Finger each chord shape using your second, third and fourth fingers and keep your first finger free to add the embellishment notes in between. Keep holding down each shape and allow the higher notes to ring out over the chord.

Example 7a

This next line includes some tense embellishments of the V chord. Here, I play a common E7#9 voicing in seventh position, which is followed by a less common E13b9 chord, voiced with its b7 (D) in the bass.

Immediately after this comes a b5 substitution, with a Bb7b5 chord replacing the E7. The Bb bass note of this chord resolves chromatically to the Am7 in bar two.

Example 7b

For the Bm7b5 in this next chord phrase, you can either fret the full chord shape and keep holding it down while you pick out the notes on beats 2 and 3 with your fingers, or you can play them as two distinct small shapes. Visualizing a shape, then picking out fragments of it is an easy way to begin to build a chord phrase.

This line uses a more colorful E7#5b9 voicing.

Example 7c

Here is a simple picked chord phrase that also contains the E7#5b9 voicing.

Example 7d

Here's a different approach. This time I've chosen to omit the Bm7b5 chord and focus just on the altered dominant 7 sound. The chord is played on beat 1 of bar one, then a cascading descending run leads to the Am9 chord in bar two.

To play the E7#5#9 chord, bar your first finger at the fifth fret, and fret the other notes with your second and fourth fingers. Remove the bar to play the descending run.

Now bar the fifth fret again and hold down the stretched Am9 shape a fraction of a second before you play the E note on beat 1 of bar two.

Example 7e

For the final three examples, we'll change key to E Minor, and the core progression will be F#m7b5 – B7 – Em7, the same chords as the minor ii V i section of *Autumn Leaves*.

In Example 7f, bar one creates the F# minor sound with an unusual chord voicing you may not have encountered before. Playing the C adjacent to the B creates a nice dissonance so let all the notes ring together as you play this chord. It also sounds great if you add in the open high E string, so check that out too.

In bar two, the simple idea is to hold down the chord shape throughout and pick out specific fragments of the chord.

In bar three we have another simple but effective idea: *delayed resolution*. Instead of resolving immediately to the Em9, the D# note on the second string is held to create lots of tension.

Example 7f

This example begins with a less common "stretched" voicing of F#m7b5. Bar your first finger at the fifth fret and hold down the full chord (with your fourth finger playing the note on the A string, fret 9) before you begin to play.

Example 7g

Here is a variation on the previous idea and uses the same F#m7b5 voicing to begin.

For the final chord, which is anticipated and played ahead of bar three, I chose another less common voicing – a spacey sounding Esus9b6. It still creates the E minor sound that we want but leaves us hanging because it sounds unresolved. It's a good chord to use if you want your arrangement to end with a twist.

Example 7h

Chapter Eight: Study Piece (based on *Yesterdays*)

Yesterdays by Jerome Kern is one of the most popular minor key jazz standards. It goes all the way back to 1933 and was written for the musical *Roberta*.

The most famous hit from that show was *Smoke Gets in Your Eyes*, but *Yesterdays* found its way into the jazz standard repertoire and remains a must-know tune. It has been recorded by all the jazz greats over the years.

Here are the chord changes that are normally played for this tune in D Minor:

| Dm7 | Em7b5 A7b9 | Dm7 | Em7b5 A7b9 |

| Dm7 Dm(Maj7)/C# | Dm7/C | Bm7b5 | E7 |

| A7#5 | D9 | G13 | C9 |

| F13 | Bbmaj7 | Em7b5 | A7b9 |

The Minor ii V i sequence is flipped around at the beginning of this tune. The I chord comes first, then the ii and V. But since it loops around, you still end up with a ii V i.

There is also a temporary or disguised minor ii V i in bars 7-8. The movement from Bm7b5 to E7 suggests a ii V in the key of A minor. Kern, however, changed the quality of the tonic from A minor to A7#5, which suggests a return to D minor, but D9 is played instead. Such twists and turns are typical of Kern's writing.

We've already seen that the idea of mixing and matching chord qualities occurs frequently in jazz harmony and is something we can use when creating our own comping lines.

Example 8a shows how I navigate bars 1-4 of the arrangement. Notice in bar three that I utilize minor 9, minor 6 and 7sus4 voicings to create a short chord phrase, mixing minor and dominant sounds.

There's also a b5 substitution in bar four, where the A7#5 chord is replaced by Eb9#11.

This substitution can be used effectively in a minor ii V i if the progression keeps looping around. So, instead of Dm7 – Em7b5 – A7#5, we can play Dm7 – Em11 – Eb9#11 with the bass notes leading chromatically back to D.

Example 8a

Later, in bars 17-20, I use different extended notes to add color to the straight D minor chord.

When it comes to bar 20, the Em7b5 chord is replaced with Bb13. This time I play a b5 substitution in place of the Em7b5, so the sequence becomes Bb13 to A7#5. You can hear that the overall harmony still remains intact, but this movement adds some nice color.

Example 8b

One of the distinguishing features of this tune occurs in bars 5-7 where, in the original, the melody ascends while the bassline descends in counterpoint. Since this is such a strong sound, highlighting the idea in our comping will help both soloists and the audience to know where we are in the tune.

Example 8c

Now here is the full comping arrangement. Have a listen to the audio first, then work through it a section at a time.

Example 8d

Cm9 C7sus4 Cm9 F7♯9 B♭add9 Em11
A7 alt Dm9 Dm6 E∅ A7♯5
Dm9 (maj7) B♭7add13 A7♯5 D5 A/C♯ F/C Gsus2/B
B♭7 F/A E/G♯ C5/G Bm7♭5 E7♯5♯9
A7♯5 D9 G13 C13
T
A
B

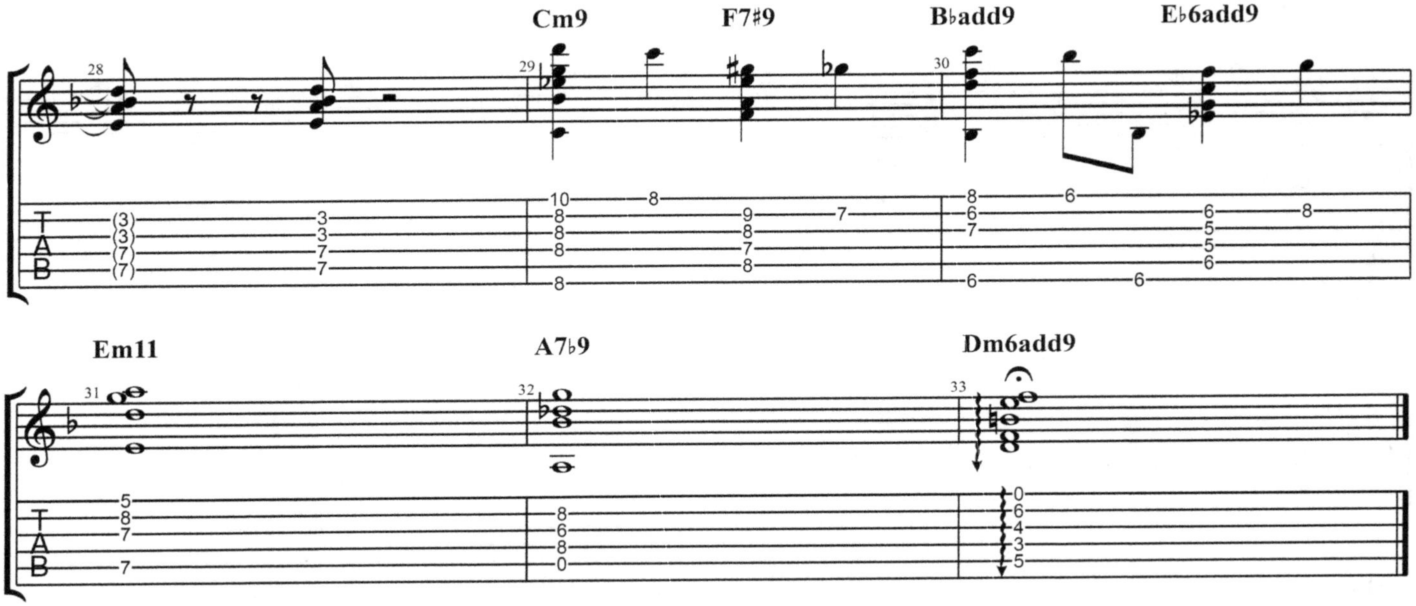
Cm9
F7♯9
B♭add9
E♭6add9
Em11
A7♭9
Dm6add9

Chapter Nine: Latin Jazz Study Piece (based on *I Remember You*)

In the introduction of this book I mentioned purchasing an album featuring Bud Shank and Laurindo Almeida, which introduced me to the music of Brazil and its rhythms. I instantly fell in love with the sound of this music and spent time studying it, eventually going on to play and record with the great Sergio Mendes and other Brazilian artists like Dori Caymmi, Toninho Horta and Ivan Lins.

Space won't allow an in-depth discussion about Latin rhythms and their use in jazz – that would take up an entire book of its own! But I can pass on some basic tips and at the end of this chapter there's a Latin-inspired comping arrangement of the tune *I Remember You* for you to learn.

I Remember You was written by Victor Shertzinger and Johnny Mercer and has been recorded in many different styles. Frank Ifield's Country version of the tune was a million selling hit record, and the song also features on The Beatles famous bootleg recording *Live! At the Star Club in Hamburg, Germany; 1962*. I played the tune on Diana Krall's album *The Look of Love* as a bossa nova.

Let's look at a few examples that will help us to build the basic Latin groove we are looking for.

When playing a Latin rhythm as an accompaniment for a soloist, it's vital to keep the pulse of the music going, so before you think of playing any complicated rhythms, you must put the bassline foundation in place.

Play through Example 9a. Notice that the bass notes fall predictably on beats 1 and 3. Play the notes with your thumb and aim to play cleanly and consistently. Work with a metronome to practice this.

This exercise may seem overly simplistic, but I can't emphasize enough how important it is to have the alternating bassline pulse locked in. We're about to add some rhythmic variation, but it's essential to keep feeling the basic pulse of the music.

Example 9a

Now we'll introduce an anticipated bass note that falls just before beat 3 of each bar.

In Example 9c we'll introduce a chord, but first I want you to mute the higher strings with your fretting hand to make a percussive sound and introduce a Latin rhythm. Before adding a chord you need to ensure the bassline is solid.

Listen to how this sounds in the audio download.

Example 9b

In Example 9c, the first bass note of each bar is now part of a full chord, and the higher strings are used for the accents.

Listen to the audio and focus on hearing the bassline, ignoring what the chord accents are doing. Can you hear that the basic pulse of the music is still tight?

The bassline is like the metronome of a Latin groove. When playing this, practice playing the bass notes a little louder than the chord accents. I play this type of pattern by plucking downward with my thumb for the bass notes and upward with my fingers for the accents.

Example 9c

Next, we're going to vary both the bassline and the accents slightly to create a two-bar pattern. As before, focus on the bassline and mute the strings to begin with to lock in this rhythm. Listen to the audio to hear how it should sound.

Example 9d

Now we're going to use this new rhythm pattern and add in some chords. To make things more interesting we'll move the chord up a half step, then back again as we loop around. Practice this with a metronome set to an easily manageable speed so that you can lock in the rhythm.

Example 9e

Next, we'll vary the chords and turn this rhythm into something that sounds much more like a song. Although played in a different key, it should sound reminiscent of *The Girl from Ipanema*.

Example 9f

The next exercise demonstrates how to apply the ideas we've looked at to a typical Brazilian-sounding chord progression.

Notice that we don't have to use complex chord forms to play this kind of music – it's possible to create the desired sound using just a few notes. It's all about the groove.

Example 9g

Finally, here is a more complex idea for you to work on during your practice sessions. Although on paper this may look more intimidating than the material we've covered so far, it's not as difficult as it seems.

In bar one, hold down these simple three-note shapes for the Em7 and A7 chords, then pick out the notes indicated in the notation. Moved these shapes down a whole step for the Dm7 to G7 movement in bar two, and another whole step for Cm7 to F7 in bar three.

From bar four onwards, it's a case of keeping the bass notes going on alternating strings while playing the chords.

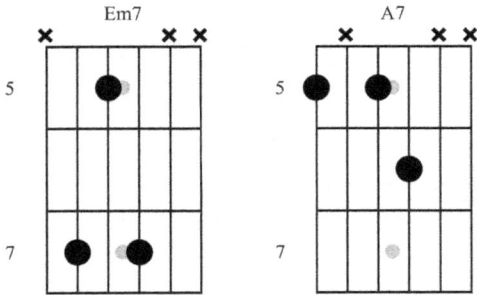

Example 9h

Now we come to the full arrangement of *I Remember You*. First, here is an overview of the chord changes most often used for this tune, which has an AABC form.

A Section:

| Ebmaj7 | Am7 D7 | Ebmaj7 | Bbm7 Eb7 |

| Abmaj7 | Abm7 Db7 | Gm7 C7 | Fm7 Bb7 |

| Ebmaj7 | Am7 D7 | Ebmaj7 | Bbm7 Eb7 |

| Abmaj7 | Abm7 Db7 | Ebmaj7 | Bbm7 Eb7 |

B Section:

| Abmaj7 | Dm7 G7 | Cmaj7 | Dm7 G7 |

| Cmaj7 | Cm7 F7 | Bbmaj7 | Fm7 Bb7 |

C Section:

| Ebmaj7 | Am7 D7 | Ebmaj7 | Bbm7 Eb7 |

| Abmaj7 | Abm7 Db7 | Gm7 C7 | Am7 D7 |

| Gm7 C7 | Fm7 Bb7 | Eb6 | Fm7 Bb7 |

Have a play through the standard chord changes to get familiar with the geography of the tune before working through the study piece.

I decided to use the first half of the A section as a kind of introduction to this arrangement (bars 1-9), played at a slower tempo. The second half of the A section, played fully up to tempo, continues at bar ten.

This comping arrangement of the tune use chords with alternating bass notes, mixed with chord phrases connected by single notes. From bar thirty-six to the end, I improvised a vamp ending for the piece. I hope you enjoy it!

Example 9i

E♭maj9
B♭m7
E♭sus4
A♭6
A♭m7
D♭7
E♭
B♭m9
E♭7♭9
A♭maj9
A7♯5
Dm11
G7add13
G7♯5
Cmaj7
Dm11
D♭9♯11
Cmaj7
Cm9
B7♭5
B♭maj7
Bmaj9
E7♭5
E♭6/9
TAB

Am11
A♭7♭5
E♭maj9
G^ø
C7♭9
TAB
Fm7
A♭m9
D♭7
Gm7
C7
TAB
G♭7♭5
Fm7
B♭/F
A♭
B♭
Fm7
B♭13♭9
TAB
E♭ 6
Bmaj7
Fm7
B♭7(♯5)
E♭6
Bmaj7
TAB

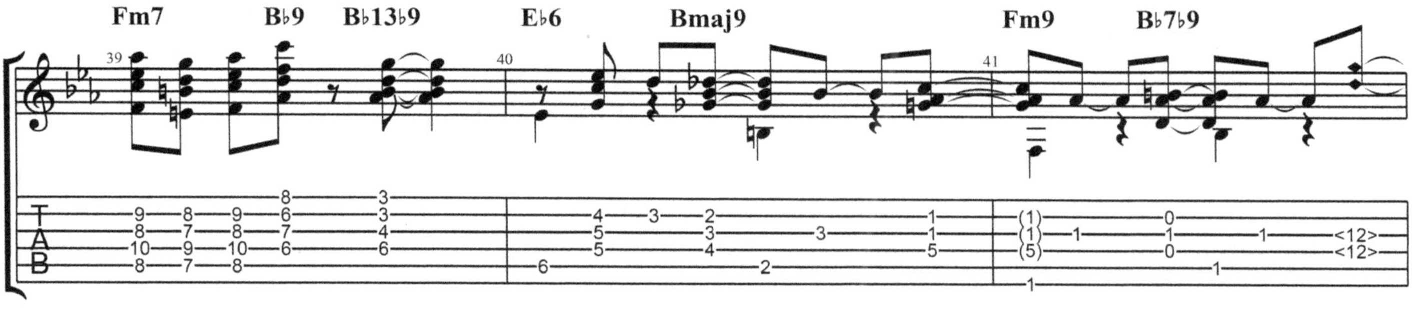
Fm7
B♭9
B♭13♭9
E♭6
Bmaj9
Fm9
B♭7♭9

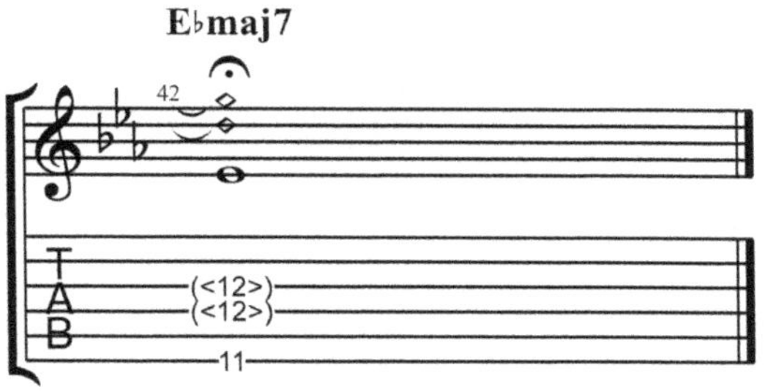
E♭maj7

Chapter Ten: Final Study (based on *All the Things You Are*)

All the Things You Are is a jam session favorite and has been used as a model for teaching jazz guitar students to comp and solo for decades.

It's another Jerome Kern tune, so it contains his trademark harmonic twists and turns, and is based around the Circle of Fifths. It's described as having an ABCD structure and here are the changes that most musicians play:

A Section:

| Fm7 | Bbm7 | Eb7 | Abmaj7 |

| Dbmaj7 | Dm7 G7 | Cmaj7 | % |

B Section:

| Cm7 | Fm7 | Bb7 | Ebmaj7 |

| Abmaj7 | Am7 D7 | Gmaj7 | % |

C Section:

| Am7 | D7 | Gmaj7 | % |

| F#m7b5 | B7b9 | Emaj7 | C7b9 |

D Section:

| Fm7 | Bbm7 | Eb7 | Abmaj7 |

| Dbmaj7 | Dbm7 | Cm7 | B°7 |

| Bbm7 | Eb7 | Abmaj7 | Gm7b5 C7b9 |

There are a few sections of the arrangement that are worthy of closer investigation before you tackle the full piece. Work through these examples and you'll have a significant part of the arrangement under your fingers.

Example 10a represents bars 13-16 of the arrangement.

In bar thirteen, the embellishment on the Abmaj7 chord demands a bit of a stretch. Fret the bass note on the low E string with your first finger, and the notes on the middle strings with your third and fourth fingers respectively.

Immediately after you've plucked the bass note, jump your first finger over onto the D string to play the descending notes, leaving your fourth finger in place.

In bars 15-16 you should be able to spot the use of the G Major harmonized chord shapes explained in Chapter One. There is also a chromatic approach chord included.

Example 10a

The next example highlights bars 32-35 of the arrangement. Notice that only the Bdim chord is played on the first beat of the bar – every other chord in this phrase is anticipated. Here, your focus should be on playing the line smoothly. It can take a little practice to play the single notes evenly while hitting the chord changes just before the beat.

Example 10b

Next, let's look at bars 40-44. There are a couple of possible ways of playing the chord phrase in bar 40.

One approach, which means moving the fretting hand as little as possible, is to start by barring the top four strings at the 3rd fret with the first finger. Now, bring the second finger over to fret the bass note on the 4th fret. This frees up the fourth finger to fret the notes on 5th fret.

Play the first triplet using the above method then, keeping your first finger barred at the 3rd fret, play the Eb note on the B string, 4th fret with the second finger, and use the fourth finger to play the embellishment notes that are available without changing position.

Break out of position to play the F on the 1st fret and reposition the fretting hand for the phrase in bar two.

Experiment with the above method and see if it works for you. Ultimately, what's right for you is what sounds good and is relatively easy for you to play.

Example 10c

This example shows bars 49-52 of the arrangement.

Perhaps one of the most challenging aspects of comping is combining straight chord playing with syncopated lines that contain embellishments. When you are providing accompaniment for a soloist, it's good to have an outline strategy of what you're going to play and what ideas you might include. You need to think ahead and avoid playing something that leads down a blind alley you can't reverse out of!

This example combines simple rhythmic chords with a ringing chord, which is followed by a syncopated, decorated line. The main goal here is to keep good time and be aware of the groove. It's no good playing something complicated if it doesn't have good time. Slow things down and practice with a metronome until you get it sounding smooth.

Example 10d

This last breakout example comes from bars 65-71 – the last section of the arrangement. It's mostly chordal, and your aim is to lock in tightly with a metronome and really punch out the syncopated chord phrases. It needs to be played with confidence!

Example 10e

Now, here is the final performance piece.

As you've done with all the previous study pieces, work through this methodically, section by section. If you find some parts tricky to negotiate, just slow things right down and focus on those sections. Break it down chord by chord if you need to, until the changes flow smoothly. I hope you enjoy these comping ideas.

Example 10f

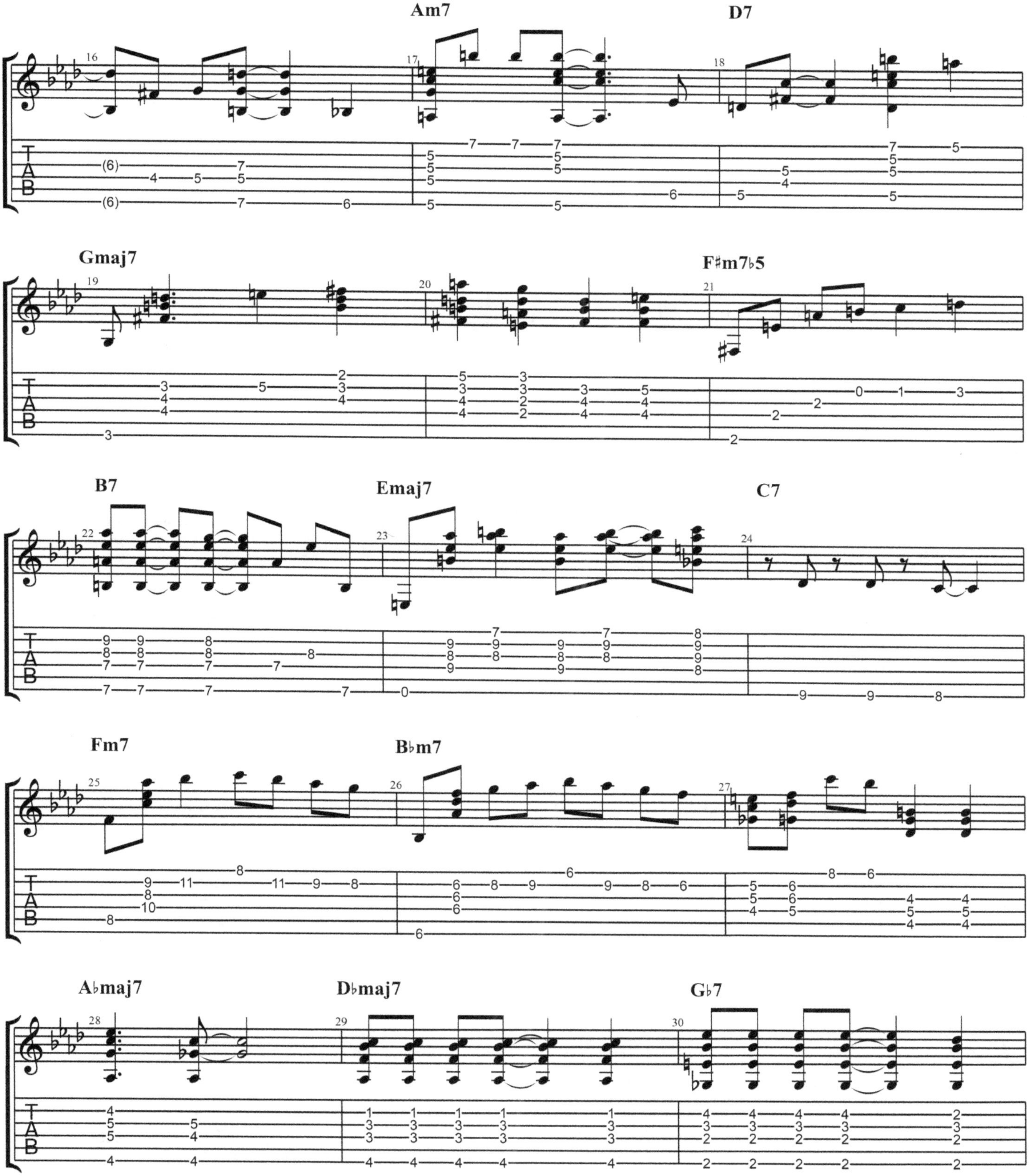
Am7
D7
Gmaj7
F♯m7♭5
B7
Emaj7
C7
Fm7
B♭m7
A♭maj7
D♭maj7
G♭7

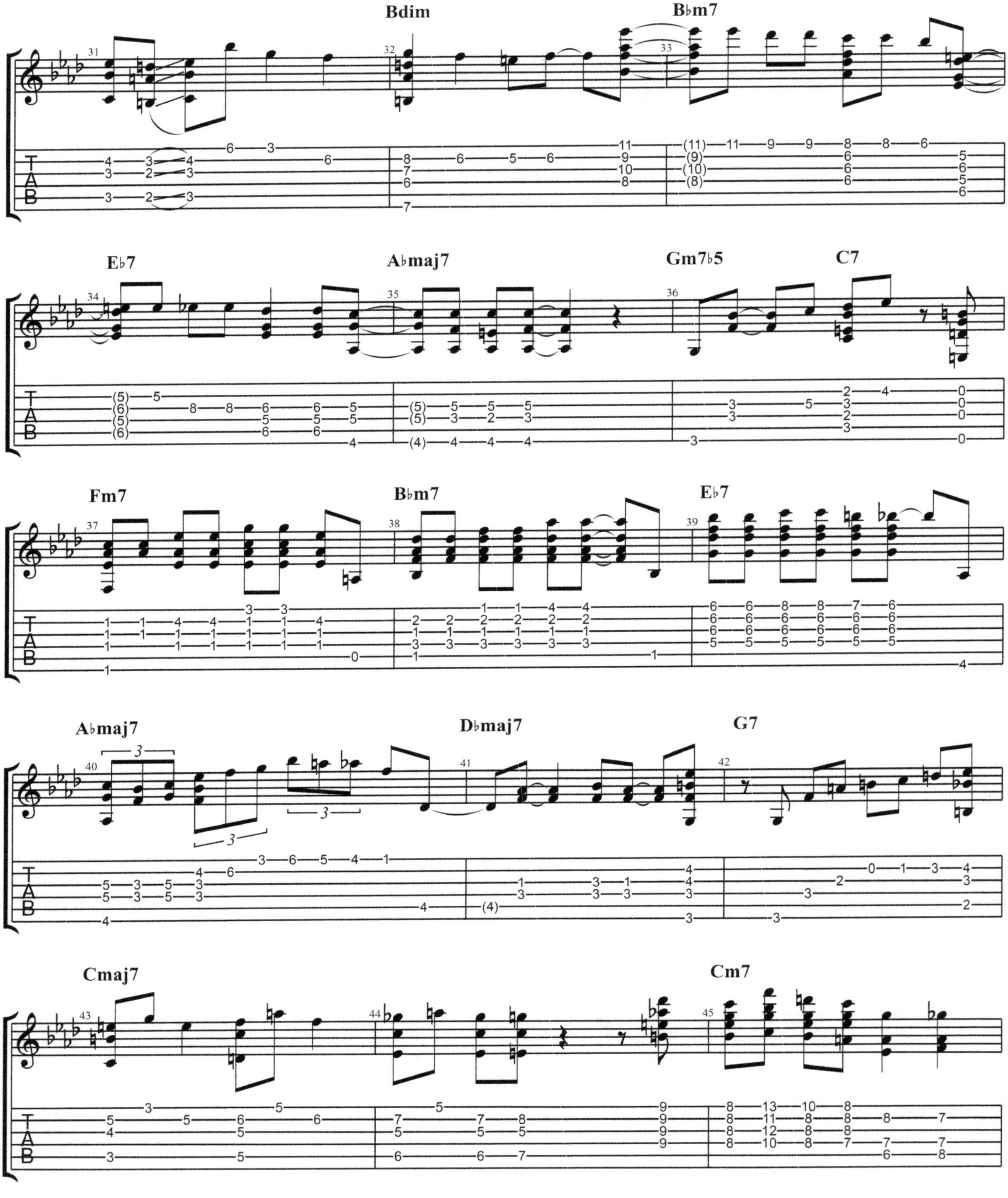
Bdim
B♭m7
E♭7
A♭maj7
Gm7♭5
C7
Fm7
B♭m7
E♭7
A♭maj7
D♭maj7
G7
Cmaj7
Cm7

Fm7
B♭7
E♭maj7
A♭maj7
Am7
D7
Gmaj7
let ring
Am
D7
A♭7
Gmaj7
F♯m7♭5
B7
Emaj7
C7

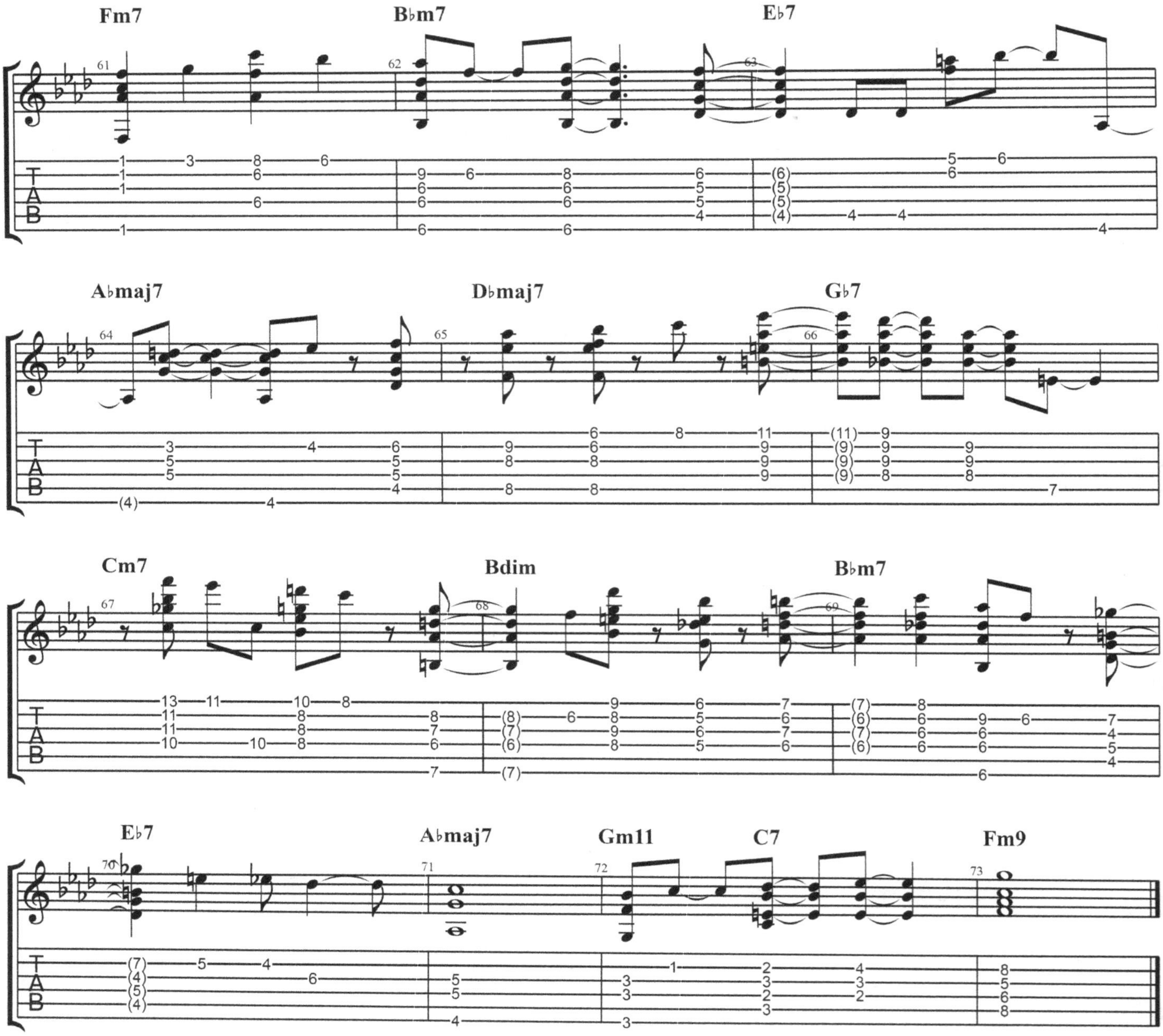
Fm7
B♭m7
E♭7
A♭maj7
D♭maj7
G♭7
Cm7
Bdim
B♭m7
E♭7
A♭maj7
Gm11
C7
Fm9

Conclusion

In this book we've looked at many different ideas to help you comp on some of the most common chord changes in jazz. I hope you've enjoyed discovering my take on these progressions and learning the longer study pieces. Now it's over to you to apply some of these ideas to your favorite tunes.

I'll leave you with a few thoughts on practicing strategies you can use to develop your comping.

1. First, I recommend diving into one of your favorite tunes – one where you are familiar with the chord progression and melody. Isolate a section of the tune (perhaps an eight-bar section, or four bars may be enough) and work on just that section to develop some comping ideas.

2. Notice where there are bars that contain just one chord. For static chords like this, practice creating movement by using other small shapes from the harmonized parent key. What connecting chords can you use that will lead to the chord in the next bar?

3. Next, look at ways in which you can make your comping more interesting by using many voicings for each chord.

4. Now write a melody line for this section of the tune. Keep it quite simple. First, try playing the melody line and chords at the same time, using appropriate voicings.

5. Next, try to harmonize the entire melody you wrote using small chord voicings. At this stage, don't worry too much about the quality of the chords. You already know the harmony of this tune well, so be guided by your ears and don't be afraid to experiment.

6. To move things along, now try moving the melody around the neck. It may be that you played it in one zone of the fretboard, so now play the melody using the range of the neck. Now, repeat the process of harmonizing the melody, so that you have an entirely different way of playing it.

7. Combine the two approaches you've created and experiment with them. Begin to work on some chord phrases that harmonize some notes, leave others as single notes, and add some bass note movement.

8. Try as many approaches as you can before you move onto the next section of the tune.

As well as practicing on your favorite tunes, listen to some big band arrangements to hear how the master arrangers, like Gil Evans, wrote and harmonized counterpoint phrases that worked with the melody. When you hear a phrase you like, work it out on guitar as a melody line, then try to harmonize it into chords. Your aim is to distil some of these ideas down onto guitar, treating it like a mini orchestra.

Also check out the recordings of players like Joe Pass, Ted Greene, Johnny Smith and Lenny Breau to hear some expert comping in action.

Above all, enjoy your musical journey!

John Pisano.

Eastman John Pisano Signature Guitar

The passion evident in John's playing extends to his attention to detail for the instruments that bear his name. From the voicing of the pickups, to the choice of carved and laminate tonewoods that make up these fine instruments, his involvement in every step of the production leads to guitars that possess not only the look, but the sound and feel worthy of this iconic musician.

Discover more at:

www.eastmanguitars.com/electric_signature_archtop

www.ingramcontent.com/pod-product-compliance
Lightning Source LLC
Chambersburg PA
CBHW081435090426

42740CB00017B/3313